Judo

MARTIAL AND FIGHTING ARTS SERIES

Judo

Jujutsu

Karate

Kickboxing

Kung Fu

Martial Arts for Athletic Conditioning

Martial Arts for Children

Martial Arts for the Mind

Martial Arts for People with Disabilities

Martial Arts for Special Forces

Martial Arts for Women

Ninjutsu

Taekwondo

JUDO

BARNABY CHESTERMAN

Senior Consultant Editor
Aidan Trimble (6th Dan)
Former World, European, and
British Karate Champion
Chairman and Chief Instructor to the
Federation of Shotokan Karate

MASON CREST PUBLISHERS
www.masoncrest.com

Introduction

When I began studying the martial arts back in 1972, the whole subject was shrouded in mystery; indeed, that was part of the attraction. At that time there was only a limited range of books on the subject and therefore very little information was available to the novice.

I am glad to say that this has changed in recent years beyond all recognition. With the explosion of interest in the martial arts and the vast array of quality books that are now on the market, we seem to be increasing our knowledge and understanding of the martial arts and sports science, and this fact is reflected in this new series of books.

Over the past 30 years, I have been privileged to compete, train, and teach with practitioners from most of the disciplines covered in this series. I have coached world champions, developed and adapted training methods for people with disabilities, and instructed members of the armed forces in close-quarter techniques. I can warmly recommend this series as a rich source of information for students and instructors alike. Books can never replace a good instructor and club, but the student who does not study when the training is finished will never progress.

Aidan Trimble—Sixth Dan, Former World Karate Champion

Judo is a Japanese martial art that has become one of the leading fighting sports throughout the world. It has been an Olympic sport since 1964 and is practiced in more countries around the world than any other sport except soccer.

A Sport and an Art

Judo is more than just a martial art; it is one of the most dynamic and spectacular of all the Olympic sports. Fighters attack with speed, agility, power, and timing, flipping their opponents high into the air and then bringing them crashing down onto the judo mat.

From there, they might roll their opponent into a hold, or force submission using an **armlock** or a strangle. That is judo at its very best. Fast, fluent, and devastating, a momentary loss of concentration can be punished in the blink of an eye. Very few will become Olympic or world champions, however. For most people, judo is not a way down the road to glory—it is a way of life. The journey may not end with a gold medal, but it does bring great rewards, friendship, and pleasure.

Judo is not an easy sport. It offers many different challenges, and is extremely physically demanding. Students learn dozens of different throwing techniques: opponents may be thrown to the front, to the rear, to the side, and even over the head. Then there are armlocks or strangles, which students learn to apply effectively, but with control, so they do not injure an opponent. Last, there are those holds that, when perfectly applied,

Judo is an Olympic sport, the roots of which are steeped in the traditions and history of a martial art. As it is more than just a sport, there is a great amount of respect and camaraderie between fighters—even at the highest level.

ARM LOCK

While judo means "the gentle way," it does include rugged techniques that can look anything but gentle. The armlock is a method of forcing a submission, but if the technique is good, applying an armlock can be as effortless as it is effective.

offer no escape. Judo students learn to link all of these techniques together to produce breathtaking moves that work both on the judo mat and in the real world.

Judo is an unarmed, close-contact martial art. It can be practiced as a means to fulfill your competitive needs, a way to get fit, or a highly effective method of self-defense. The throws, holds, strangles, and armlocks of judo offer its students a wide variety of skills.

Contrary to what most people believe, each type of martial art is quite different, and each has its own unique brand of techniques. For instance, judo is absolutely nothing like karate. You cannot punch, kick, or chop in judo, but the skills you learn are just as effective and spectacular. As an art form, judo can enrich the lives of those who practice it through self-fulfillment, achievement, and the friendships gained throughout the worldwide judo family.

As a sport, only soccer is practiced in a greater number of countries. At the 2000 Olympic Games, in Sydney, Australia, more countries fielded an athlete in judo than in any other sport. All over the world, in countries as diverse as Estonia in Northern Europe and Cuba in the Caribbean, judo champions are some of the national favorite sporting heroes.

What makes judo truly special, however, is that it can fulfill a wide variety of needs. Whatever your age and whatever your level, there is always a place for you on the judo mat. And for the elite athletes, there is always the ultimate aim of Olympic glory.

A BIT OF HISTORY

Before you begin to study judo, it is useful to have an appreciation of its history and roots. Although judo literally means "the gentle way," its techniques are derived from the battlefields of **feudal** Japan. Indeed, the term "martial art" really refers to skills used on the battlefield. The martial arts were developed from close-quarter fighting methods used during wartime.

The Japanese martial arts were mostly developed during the feudal period (in the 17th century) by the **samurai** and warrior classes. One such art was jujutsu, one of the deadliest forms of open-handed combat. It was from this art that judo was born.

Jigoro Kano, the founder of judo, began as a student of jujutsu. He was born on October 28, 1860, in a small village in Japan called Mikage, which is now in the East Nada district of the city of Kobe. His family consisted of

Jigoro Kano, the founder of judo, was an incredible man who not only spread judo throughout the world, but also pushed Japan onto the international sporting arena.

wealthy brewers who made **sake**, a traditional type of distilled wine. Kano was a frail boy with a quick temper. He grew up eager to learn about how the weak could overcome the strong. It was this interest that formed the basis for his development of judo. He defined judo as having two mottos: "seiryoku zenyo," which means "make the most efficient and positive use of your physical and spiritual energies"; and "jita kyoei," which means "live in harmony and prosperity with others."

The first motto essentially means that judo is about getting the maximum amount of efficiency from the minimum amount of effort. That is why Kano called it "the gentle way"; it is about giving in to an opponent's force, rather than struggling against him or her in order to win the fight. A simple way of looking at the principle of "giving in" to your opponent is to imagine that someone is pushing you. You do not push back; instead, you use his or her force against him or her by moving yourself out of the pushing line. Without the resistance of your body to push against, your opponent will become unbalanced, making it easy to guide him or her down to the floor. For example, if you were to push as hard as you could against a wall, and then suddenly someone took the wall away, you would, of course, fall over. This is how Kano envisaged the weak overcoming the strong.

The second of Kano's mottos relates to the fulfillment and spiritual sides of judo. Those who practice judo often become more confident and self-assured, which can help them in their daily lives. Even though judo is a competitive fighting art, when you join a judo club, you will probably make friends with the other students there. During the practice sessions, you will fight against each other within the sporting rules of judo. Although competitive judo involves a "fight," the competition actually brings the

A EUROPEAN CONTENDER

Almost every single country now has its own judo association—even tiny Pacific islands like Tonga. Although the Japanese initially dominated their own sport, the Europeans quickly caught up. The great giant Dutchman Anton Geesink caused a shock in 1961 when he became the first non-Japanese world champion. He also won the first open-category Olympic title. Wilhelm Ruska, another Dutchman, followed in Geesink's footsteps, also becoming a world and Olympic champion.

Once judo had spread throughout the world, challenge matches were arranged between representative teams from different countries. It was soon obvious that an international body would have to be set up in order to provide standardized competition rules. In 1948, the post-war European Judo Union was formed. In 1951, Argentina applied for membership, and the organization changed its name to become the International Judo Federation. That same year, the first post-war European Judo championships were held in Paris, France, and a year later, the first Pan-American championships took place in Havana, Cuba. In 1956, the first World Championships were held in Japan. Judo was introduced into the Olympic program in 1964.

Over the years, many different countries have produced judo champions. While many sports are dominated by an elite group of individuals or countries, judo is truly a world sport. Countries on every continent have produced either a world or Olympic champion, including some from such diverse places as Venezuela, Azerbaijan, Tunisia, and North Korea. Even Belgium, one of the smallest countries in Europe, has produced three of the finest female **judo-ka** people who practice judo) ever, and former Soviet republics, like Georgia and Uzbekistan, boast some of the most feared fighters in the world. The U.S. has also produced both male and female world champions. Of course, no one can match the achievements of the Japanese in the judo category of both the world and Olympic championships.

Judo may not be the most popular sport in the world, nor the most televised or the most glamorous, but for sheer excitement, drama, and level of unpredictability, it is unsurpassed. Furthermore, there is no finer activity to pursue for a physical, mental, and spiritual education.

Focus and concentration are vital in judo competition. Here, the U.S.'s Amy Tong prepares herself mentally before a bout.

The Basic Elements of Judo

As with any traditional martial art, there is a lot more to judo than just getting out there and wrestling or sparring. The sport is steeped in tradition and history, a fact that is reflected in the place at which judo is practiced. This place is called the dojo, which literally means "a place to learn the way."

The **dojo** will usually consist of anything from 40 to 100 **tatami** (special rectangular judo mats), depending on the size of the hall. Traditional mats were made of straw and mounted on a springy wooden floor. Today, mats are made of synthetic material and tend to just be laid down on the floor of a sports hall or club.

Most dojos contain objects of respect, such as a photo of Jigoro Kano and other judo dignitaries, or a calligraphy drawing of a judo-related motto. These objects are placed at the far end of the dojo. As a mark of respect, you should bow to them as you enter the dojo. You should also bow when you step on and off the mat and as you leave.

This bowing, or "**rai**," as it is known, is important in a tough physical martial art. It is done as a sign of friendship and respect for your practice

With perfect timing and technique, judo looks effortless. Here, the great Japanese world and Olympic champion, Toshihiko Koga, throws his opponent over his head despite having only a minimal grip on his opponent's uniform.

THE BOW

The bow in judo holds great significance. It is a mark of respect and friendship. Students bow to the instructor at the beginning of a class and to each other before every practice.

partner and to diffuse any tension that may build up during practice. The bow can be done either from a standing position, by bending at the waist, or from a kneeling position, by bending forward, lowering your head, and placing both hands on the mat.

Not all judo schools insist on traditional forms of etiquette, but the instructor should always be treated with the utmost respect, as he or she is responsible for your safety, well-being, and education inside the dojo. Some instructors insist on being called "sensei," which means instructor; whereas some like to keep sessions informal, letting you call them by their first names. It all depends on the instructor, but it is always best to call him or her sensei—unless, of course, he or she specifically asks you not to.

THE JUDO UNIFORM

The traditional judo uniform is a thick, white, cotton "**judogi**," or judo suit. The judo suit consists of pants and an open jacket with a thick collar. Professional fighters often buy tight-fitting, tailor-made suits with especially thick collars. Such uniforms make it difficult for opponents to get a grip on their jackets, thus giving themselves every possible advantage in competition.

In competition, one fighter wears a white judogi, and the other, a blue one. This change was made in the mid-1990s to make judo more aesthetically pleasing to the public. (On television, it is much easier to distinguish between two bodies flying through the air if one is wearing a dark suit and the other a light one). The difference in uniforms also helps the referees, as it is a lot easier to award a score to a fighter when you can clearly see which color hit the mat first.

The judo suit is particularly tough—much tougher than that worn for any other martial art. Judo-ka use great force to pull each other around, and often use the opponent's jacket or pants for leverage. Therefore, the uniform must be able to withstand aggressive treatment.

It is essential that students of judo keep their uniforms clean, as personal hygiene is extremely important. You should always wash before practicing on the judo mat. If you do not, you will make training unpleasant for your practice partners, as you will often be rolling around in close contact. You should also make sure that your nails are clean and always kept short, and you should remove any jewelry (rings that cannot be removed should be taped to the finger). This is both for your own protection and for that of your partner.

BELT TYING

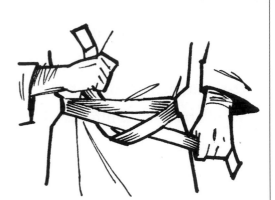

STEP 1: The belt is held at the front before crossing the ends over at the back and pulling them back to the front.

STEP 2: The left end is looped under the right end.

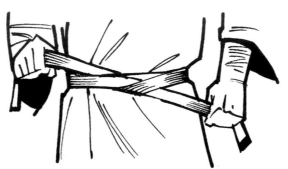

STEP 3: And then pulled tight.

STEP 4: Loop the left end under the right end again to form a double knot.

STEP 5: The completed belt.

THE GRADING SYSTEM

The judo suit is tied closed using a thick, cotton, colored belt. The color of the belt denotes the person's grade: white or red are beginner colors, and black is for experts. The coveted black belt has a special aura about it because it demonstrates that you have reached an important milestone in this martial art.

However, many judo masters believe that the black belt is only the beginning. According to these masters, once you have attained the grade of black belt, or 1st "**dan**," only then are you ready to really start learning about judo.

The black belt grades run in ascending order, with 1st dan being the lowest and 11th dan the highest. Theoretically, there is no limit to the number of dans that can be awarded, but Jigoro Kano only reached 11th dan, and so no one else has ever been awarded anything above 10th dan. Therefore, realistically, 10th dan is the highest grade that can be attained. Below the black belt, the grades are called **kyus**. Kyus run in descending order: 10th kyu denotes a complete beginner, while 1st kyu is just below 1st dan.

In Japan, judo-ka wear a white belt for all the kyu grades, but in Western countries, different-colored belts are awarded for different grades. The exact sequence of colored belts depends on the particular country and association, but the order tends to go: white, yellow, orange, green, blue, and then brown.

Judo is a particularly tough martial art because it is one of the few in which you are required to fight contests in order to progress up the grades. You can attain higher grades by simply completing the theory and successfully demonstrating techniques, but your progress will be a lot slower than those who are successful in grading contests.

COMPETITIVE JUDO

Some people merely practice judo for enjoyment or to get fit. But for those who want to enter competitions or try to make it onto a regional or national squad, they need to learn how to fight competitively. Competitive judo is about winning, and there are certain tricks of the trade that you can learn to gain a winning advantage. Those who enter competitions also need to be aware of the various rules, scoring, and penalties. (Competitive judo is also covered in the training section, starting on page 81).

GRIPPING

Gripping is an important part of judo, as a fighter who manages to dominate the grip will be in a much stronger position to throw his or her opponent. The traditional grip for a right-handed fighter is to put your right hand on your opponent's opposite lapel and your left hand on his opposite sleeve. You can either grip the sleeve near the elbow, or you can grip it at the end. Some fighters will hold both sleeves.

There are several variations to the grip that can help you gain an advantage; for example, holding your opponent's collar around the back of his or her neck, rather than at the lapel, is a strong grip used by attack-minded fighters. Another tactic is to hold both lapels or to have one hand on the lapel and the other on the collar. The key is to find something you feel comfortable gripping. You can grip anywhere on the jacket, pants, and belt, although there are time restrictions for gripping the pants and the belt.

GRIPPING

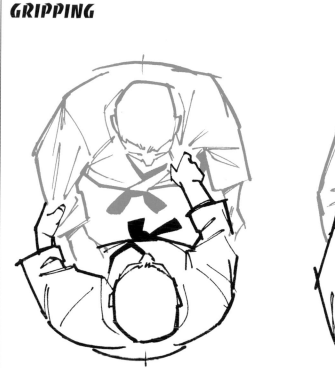

CONVENTIONAL RIGHT-HANDED GRIP: The student holds his opponent's lapel with his right hand and sleeve with his left.

DOUBLE-LAPEL GRIP: This allows the student to pull his opponent in closer, giving greater power to his throws.

DOUBLE-SLEEVE GRIP: This allows the student more space between him and his opponent and gives him more room to maneuver in the space between them.

BREAK-FALLS

Before you can even begin to practice judo, you must first learn to fall—not necessarily gracefully, but safely. Judo is not a sport like boxing, where you can just walk into a gym and start hammering a punching bag. It can be quite dangerous, so learning to fall without hurting yourself is important.

There are four types of break-falls, or "ukemi," as they are known: forward, backward, sideways, and rolling. The forward break-fall begins in a standing position. You then let your body fall forwards and land on your forearms. You must take the impact on your forearms rather than on your hands to avoid damaging your wrists. A backward break-fall is done by simply squatting and then rolling backwards, slapping the mat by your sides with outstretched arms. From the same squatting position, you can perform the sideways break-fall. Stretch out one leg and flop down to that side, slapping the mat by your side with your arm as you land. The rolling break-fall is just like a forward roll, except that it is done over one shoulder rather than straight over your head. Whichever shoulder you use, you should slap the mat with your other arm as you land on your back.

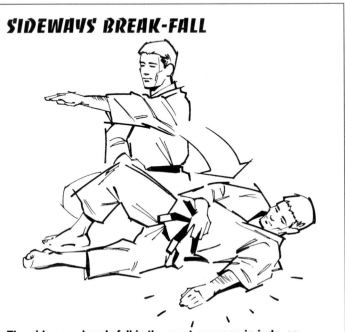

SIDEWAYS BREAK-FALL

The sideways break-fall is the most common in judo, as throws are usually done holding one of the opponent's arms. Here, the impact is taken on the full length of the arm.

BACKWARD AND FORWARD BREAK-FALLS

BACKWARD BREAK-FALL: The student sits back on her bottom and slaps the mat on either side of her with the full length of both arms.

FORWARD BREAK-FALL: The impact is taken only on the forearms. The student falls forward, but keeps her hips and head off the mat and lands on her forearms.

THE RULES

Modern judo consists of three main elements: throws, holds, and submissions. Submissions consist of strangles, or chokes, which apply pressure to the throat area, and armlocks, which apply pressure to the elbow joint. When Kano originally devised judo, he also included striking techniques as well as various other locks to the neck, back, and legs, but these have been banned in contemporary judo for safety reasons. They are still practiced and demonstrated by high-ranking masters in traditional forms of **kata**.

You score points in a judo contest in one of three ways: throwing an opponent to the ground; pinning his or her back to the mat for a certain amount of time; or forcing a submission by applying either an armlock or a strangle. To submit to your opponent, tap him or her a few times with an open hand. If your arms are tied up, making it impossible for you to tap your opponent, you can either tap the mat with your foot or, if you are really desperate, just scream. If your opponent submits, you should always release him or her immediately.

SCORING

There are four different scores awarded in judo: **ippon**, which is a full-point score and ends the contest immediately, like a knock-out in boxing; **waza-ari**, which is a half-point score (two of these equal an ippon); **yuko**; and **koka**. (Yuko and koka are not worth anything in numeric terms. They are both small scores, of which yuko is the higher).

Judo focuses on quality rather than on the quantity or the sum of scores. Thus, one higher score will always beat two or more lower scores added together. For example, one waza-ari score triumphs over yuko and koka—

When two fighters attack each other with full commitment, it can result in some spectacular action. Here, both fighters need to be able to break their landing, as both bodies have been launched into the air.

or any number of either. Likewise, yuko triumphs over any number of koka scores. The ippon automatically ends a contest, as do two waza-ari scores, but no number of yuko or koka scores can end a contest before its regulation finish.

To make things easier for the public to understand, numeric values were given to the four scores, but these can actually confuse matters. An ippon is worth 10 points; waza-ari is worth seven; yuko is worth five; and koka is worth three. But two seven-point waza-ari scores equal one 10-point ippon, and five three-point koka scores are less than two five-point yuko scores. Clearly, the point system can cause more confusion than it solves. To experienced judo practitioners, this system makes sense, but to outsiders, it can be quite complicated.

To score ippon, you must throw your opponent mainly on his or her back with speed and control, pin your opponent for 25 seconds, or force a submission. To score waza-ari, your throw must be partially lacking one of the three elements necessary to score an ippon; you can also score by pinning your opponent down for 20 seconds. Yuko is scored when a throw is partially lacking two of the elements necessary for an ippon; it can also be scored for a hold of 15 seconds. Koka is scored for a throw that causes your opponent to tumble onto the mat partially on his or her back; it can also be awarded for a hold of 10 seconds.

PENALTIES

There are equivalent penalty scores awarded for various prohibited acts, which equate to the same values as the actual scores. **Shido** is equivalent to koka; **chui**, to yuko; **keikoku**, to waza-ari; and hansoku-make is a disqualification equal to ippon.

Penalties work differently than the scores, however, in that they are cumulative. This means that if you have already been penalized chui, you cannot receive a shido or another chui. If you were to receive another penalty, your cumulative penalty score would become keikoku. One more penalty after that would result in a disqualification.

To score the maximum ippon with a throw, a competitor must throw his opponent flat on his back with impetus and control. Kyrgyzstan's Bazarbek Donbay wins bronze at the Sydney 2000 Olympics with just such a throw.

There is a whole range of prohibited acts that will earn penalties. Some of these are designed to protect either you or your opponent, while others are designed to encourage an attack in order to engage the audience. Some of the prohibited acts are:

- Any form of strike or illegal joint-lock
- Deliberately stepping out of the competition area
- Holding on to your opponent's belt for more than five seconds without attacking
- Dropping to your knees without attempting a throw

AGE AND SAFETY

Some judo techniques are prohibited to certain age groups during contests. It is useful to know exactly which ones these are and the ages that are forbidden to perform them, so that you do not do them by accident in a contest. For example, for safety reasons, children under 16 are not allowed to perform submission techniques in competition, although they are occasionally taught some of these techniques during training. Kanabasame (scissor-throw) is a technique that was banned towards the end of the 20th century because, although a highly effective throw, when done improperly, it can cause damage to your opponent's knees. From personal experience, I once twisted my knee when an opponent attempted a poorly executed kanabasame on me. So, for safety reasons, it is now banned.

- Ducking underneath your opponent's arm
- Putting fingers up your opponent's sleeve or pant leg
- Attempting to throw while applying a submission technique
- Head-diving

Most of these moves will automatically be penalized shido, but certain actions carry heavier penalties. Head-diving (when a thrower drives his or her head down towards the mat while attempting a fully committed throw), for example, earns hansoku-make (disqualification). Head-diving is dangerous for the thrower and can result in a serious neck injury, given that the thrower's opponent lands on top of him or her. Sergio Domenech of Spain was a recent high-profile casualty of head-diving when he broke his neck performing this act in March 2000.

THE JUDO CONTEST

Tournament bouts take place in a competition area of either 25 ft by 25 ft (8 m by 8 m) or 33 ft by 33 ft (10 m by 10 m). There is a red outer ring within this area known as the "danger area" (hence the color red), which warns fighters that they are approaching the edge of the mat. Unlike **sumo** wrestling, however, there is a safety area about 9 ft (3 m) wide around the edge of the mat. A throw that lands outside the contest area can score as long as it started inside the safety area.

Each contest has three judges. There is a central referee, who moves around inside the contest area, and two corner judges, who sit just outside the contest area. The referee scores each bout, but the two corner judges can overrule his or her decision if they are in agreement that he or she made a mistake on a call. There are five minutes of actual fighting time in a contest, and the clock is stopped when there is a break in the action. Junior contests usually last three minutes, but if the participants are older, a contest may last for four or five minutes.

The timekeeper sits at a table at the side of the mat. The scoreboard will either be on the table or next to it, where it is clearly visible for both the fighters and the audience.

Competitors can have a coach sitting by the side of the mat. Many coaches, particularly the top ones, are quite animated, often barking instructions at their weary fighters.

The coach actually has an important role to play during a competition, as it can be difficult for a competitor to recognize his or her mistakes during a contest, and they rely on their coach

Coaches play a vital role during judo contests, motivating their fighters and barking out tactics and instructions. Cuba's Ronaldo Veitia Valdivie is as famous around the world as any fighter.

to tell them where they are going wrong. The coaches also tend to play a significant role in trying to sway the referee's decisions.

Although Kano's principle in developing judo was that the weak should be able to overcome the strong, in international competitions, a 133lb (60kg) fighter has little chance against a 220lb (100kg) opponent. It is one thing to overcome a much bigger, heavier attacker in the street who has no knowledge of martial arts, but it is quite another to beat a heavier, stronger opponent who trains as hard as you and who may be one of the best fighters in his or her country. So for fairness and equality of competition, judo is split into seven different weight categories for both men and women. The lightest men's category is under 133lb (60kg), and the heaviest is over 220lb (100kg). For women, the range is from under 106lb (48kg) to over 172lb (78kg).

The different weight categories actually help make judo an interesting spectator sport. A contest between two lightweights will be quite different from one between two middleweights or two heavyweights. Your height, weight, and build all have a bearing on what type of technique will suit you best. In the lightweight and middleweight categories, fighters have the strength to lift each other using big pick-up techniques. But when two 310lb (140kg) fighters get together, they simply do not have the explosive speed and power necessary to lift each other cleanly off the mat.

Similarly, men's and women's judo differ substantially. Women tend not to have the same upper-body strength as men, but, because they are generally shorter, their center of gravity is usually lower. This is why women tend to favor leg rather than arm techniques. All of these differences make for fascinating viewing at competitions.

Judo Techniques

The basis of any martial art is the techniques it encompasses. And like all the martial arts, judo techniques exude effectiveness. Whether it is the dynamism of throws, the stifling holds or the uncompromising submissions—judo techniques are brutally efficient and effective, both on the mat and in the street. This chapter examines the key techniques of the sport and what you can learn from them.

Judo techniques are split into four categories: tachi-waza (throwing techniques), osaekomi-waza (pinning techniques), shime-waza (strangles and chokes), and kansetsu-waza (armlocks). When learning judo, you will discover a variety of these techniques and you will also be taught how to link them together.

Together, the four categories encompass the entire range of close-combat maneuvers that you would need in a self-defense situation. Throws are the most impressive techniques and also the most important to learn, as fights always begin in a standing position. But once a competitive bout, or indeed a self-defense situation, moves onto the ground, that is when the other three categories become vital.

When a judo throw is executed perfectly, it can be one of the most dramatic sights in sport. Japan's incomparable Kosei Inoue is totally committed to this throw and does not even have one toe touching the mat at this point.

The great Toshihiko Koga of Japan throwing with a two-handed shoulder throw on his way to the world title in 1995. He had incredible spring in his legs and could flip much heavier opponents over his head.

is not one of the more traditional Japanese techniques. In fact, its sister technique, morote-seoi-nage (the two-armed shoulder throw), is the more traditional of the shoulder throws. The one-armed shoulder throw is, however, more commonly used in competitive judo because of its greater versatility.

The conventional way to perform the one-armed shoulder throw is to take hold of your opponent's right sleeve with your left hand. Hold the sleeve around the elbow, as this will enable you to get a strong pulling action in towards your body. It is conventional practice to begin by holding the sleeve and lapel of your opponent as in the standard grip, so as not to telegraph your intentions. But to actually do the throw, you need to let go with one hand.

Throw your right arm underneath your opponent's right armpit as you step forward with your right foot. Place your right foot in between your

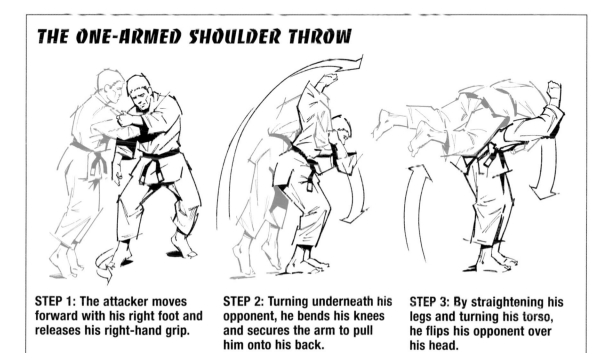

THE ONE-ARMED SHOULDER THROW

STEP 1: The attacker moves forward with his right foot and releases his right-hand grip.

STEP 2: Turning underneath his opponent, he bends his knees and secures the arm to pull him onto his back.

STEP 3: By straightening his legs and turning his torso, he flips his opponent over his head.

opponent's legs and in line with your own left foot. Then, pivot on the ball of your right foot as you twist your body around to face the same direction as your opponent. At the same time, move your left foot and place it next to your own right foot—with both feet facing away from your opponent—while bending your knees. This will drop your center of gravity below that of your opponent's.

As you twist your body, pull sharply with your left hand so that your right bicep is pressed tightly underneath your opponent's armpit. By bending your right elbow, you should be able to keep your opponent's right arm trapped. This will prevent him or her from escaping as you execute the throw. Now bend forward slightly and straighten your legs; you will see that you can now lift your opponent off the ground and onto your back. Complete the throw by rotating your head and body to the left, so that your

THE BODY DROP

STEP 1: The attacker breaks his opponent's balance by forcing him to step forward to his right.

STEP 2: He then swivels his body to face the same way as his opponent by pivoting on his right foot.

STEP 3: He then completes the throw by stepping across his opponent's right leg and pulling him over it.

opponent is thrown over your right shoulder and onto his or her back. When throwing a partner during practice, it is important to always keep a hold of his or her sleeve to help break his or her fall.

In competition, this throw is often executed by doing a complete somersault with your opponent on your back. This is the kind of strength and commitment needed to throw someone at the highest level. The result is a visually spectacular technique, with two bodies flying through the air.

You can also perform this type of throw holding your opponent's lapel instead of his or her sleeve. This method will give you more control and power, but will make it more difficult to rotate your body. It is also easier to defend against.

When performing the two-armed shoulder throw, keep hold of your opponent's lapel with your right hand, and bend your right elbow underneath his or her right armpit rather than throwing your whole arm under the armpit. This method can also be done with both hands grabbing his or her right lapel and sleeve, and is generally more powerful than the one-armed shoulder throw.

TAI-OTOSHI: THE BODY DROP

The body drop is usually one of the first techniques taught to juniors, particularly in Japan, where it is regarded as one of the more classical techniques. It is ideal for short, stocky fighters who can easily form a low stance. The secret to effective application of this technique is in the grip. A conventional right-handed grip is used, but unlike the shoulder throw, the left hand should hold your opponent's sleeve as low as possible, rather than by the elbow. Grabbing the sleeve low will allow you to get a strong pull across your body. It will also give you more control over your opponent's right hand. If you pull down on your opponent's sleeve, you can stop him or her from grabbing your lapel using his or her right hand, giving you a big advantage.

From the conventional right-handed grip, take a step forward with your right foot, just as with the shoulder throw. Pivot on the ball of that foot, and turn your body to your left, so that you are facing the same direction as your opponent. At the same time, step outwards with your left foot and place it outside your opponent's left leg. Then, drop your center of gravity by stepping your right leg across your opponent's right leg and planting it firmly on the mat, slightly bent, with the back of your knee resting against your opponent's shin. Twist your head and body to your left while pulling your opponent's sleeve across your body, and drive your right hand (which is holding your opponent's lapel) forwards. At the same time, straighten your right leg. This will push the back of your knee against your opponent's shin, and will knock his or her feet off the ground. With his or her balance broken, your rotation will pull him or her over your hip and spin him or her onto his or her back.

This technique is equally effective when done from a grip with both hands on the same side. The important thing to remember is to sink your hips as low as possible to get underneath your opponent's center of gravity.

The seoi-toshi (shoulder drop) is similar to the body drop. This technique combines the grips and hand movements from the shoulder throws and the leg action from the body drop. The shoulder drop is an effective combination technique to attempt after a shoulder throw has been blocked. If an opponent is pulling backwards and blocking the shoulder throw, you

THE FLOATING DROP

STEP 1: The attacker breaks his opponent's balance forward by swiveling his left foot around behind his right.

STEP 2: By pulling down hard on his opponent's right sleeve and pushing up with his own right hand, his opponent stumbles forward.

STEP 3: By continuing the steering-wheel motion with his hands, his opponent is forced to somersault onto his back.

can simply drop your hips and spread your legs in the body-drop position to take him or her over your hip rather than over your shoulder.

UKI-OTOSHI: THE FLOATING DROP

The floating drop is a traditional judo technique that epitomizes the principle of using an opponent's momentum against him or her. It is mostly a demonstration technique, as it is quite difficult to perform in competition.

This technique is performed from a conventional right-handed grip. Take a circular backwards step with your left leg behind your right leg, pulling sharply with your left hand on your opponent's sleeve. This will force him or her to take a step forward with his right leg, thus breaking his balance to his front right corner. As your opponent tries to regain his or her balance by taking a step forward with his or her right foot, drop onto your left knee, and make a steering-wheel motion with your hands, pulling upwards with your right and downwards with your left. Your opponent will now have flipped over his or her own right shoulder and will have landed on his or her back.

This is the kind of technique that looks effortless and spectacular to outsiders, but is difficult to perform, requiring perfect timing. It is not an effective competition throw, as it requires perfect technique and no strength.

With sweeping techniques, the attacker whisks his opponent's feet out from under him. Here, Belgium's Harry Van Barneveld throws his Turkish opponent with a knee-wheel technique, hiza-guruma.

ASHI-WAZA: THE FOOT-SWEEP TECHNIQUES

Foot-sweeps are entirely unique to judo. Although Jigoro Kano was a student of jujutsu and derived judo from its sister art, jujutsu contains no foot-sweeps of any kind. Neither does aikido. Therefore, foot-sweeps were entirely the brainchild of Kano himself.

Foot-sweeps also perfectly encompass Kano's principle of the weak overcoming the strong through minimal force. To illustrate, by simply sweeping away your opponent's stepping foot just before he places his or her weight on it, you can send him or her crashing down to the floor with the slightest of movements on your part.

In fact, the effort is so small that, when being thrown with a foot-sweep, you tend to feel

MAJOR OUTER FOOT-SWEEP

STEP 1: The attacker steps past her opponent with her left leg, leaning her opponent over.

STEP 2: She swings her right leg through the gap between her left leg and her opponent.

STEP 3: And then sweeps her right leg away, making sure that she leans forward throughout the technique.

helpless and embarrassed at how little effort your opponent needed to send you tumbling down to the mat.

O-SOTO-GARI: MAJOR OUTER FOOT-SWEEP

The major outer foot-sweep is one of the most commonly used techniques in competitive judo. It is a powerful throwing method, particularly for tall, strong fighters. It can be done from a conventional right-handed grip, but it is more powerful from a high right-handed grip around the back of the opponent's neck.

To perform this technique, break your opponent's balance to his or her front right corner by pulling down with your left hand. This will force him or her to take a small step forward with his or her right foot. At the same time, step forward with your left foot, placing it outside and parallel to your opponent's right foot. Leaning forwards, swing your right leg between your left leg and your opponent's right leg. Now sweep away your opponent's right leg as you swing your right leg back, hitting the back of his or her right knee with the back of your own calf. As you swing your leg backwards, lean forwards—this action will help to drive your opponent backwards and to the ground.

The major outer foot-sweep is similar to an o-soto-gake (major outer hook). In the hooking technique, your right leg is used to block your opponent's left ankle, and you throw him or her by driving him or her backwards with your arms. A couple of other throws from the same group are ko-soto-gari (minor outer foot-sweep) and ko-soto-gake (minor outer hook). With these techniques, you sweep or hook the leg opposite your own attacking leg, thus attacking your opponent's left leg rather than his or her right leg.

O-UCHI-GARI: MAJOR INNER FOOT-SWEEP

The major inner foot-sweep is not just an attacking technique; it is also a popular setup technique when you plan to follow up with a different attack. The major inner foot-sweep is done from a conventional right-handed grip, and the principle is similar to that of the outer foot-sweep. This time, however, you break your opponent's balance to his or her front left corner by pulling with your right hand. This will make him or her step forward with his or her left leg, which is the one you want to sweep.

To perform this technique, step forward with your left foot and place it between and just in front of your opponent's legs. Swing your right leg between your opponent's legs in a

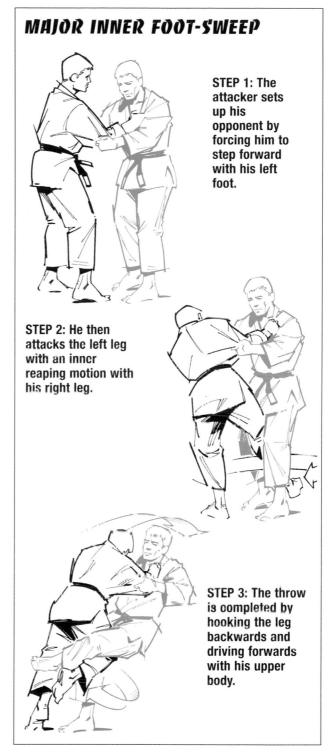

MAJOR INNER FOOT-SWEEP

STEP 1: The attacker sets up his opponent by forcing him to step forward with his left foot.

STEP 2: He then attacks the left leg with an inner reaping motion with his right leg.

STEP 3: The throw is completed by hooking the leg backwards and driving forwards with his upper body.

circular motion, and sweep his or her left leg in the same way as you would sweep his or her right leg in the major foot-sweep: by knocking the back of his or her knee with the back of your calf. The inner foot-sweep has the same sweeping and hooking variations as the outer foot-sweep.

HIZA-GURUMA: KNEE WHEEL

While most foot-sweep techniques use the foot to sweep or block the opponent's ankle, the knee wheel attacks a higher point. It is ideally suited to a scenario in which an opponent is stepping towards you. Apart from the two foot-sweeps previously described, most foot-sweeps use a lot of arm and upper-body rotation. The knee wheel is one such technique.

From a conventional right-handed grip, break your opponent's balance by pulling down and to the left, with your left hand, and pushing up and to the left with your right, in a steering-wheel motion. This will force your opponent to take a step with his or her right foot. But before he or she can do so, raise your left foot to block just below his or her knee. Simultaneously, start to rotate your body around to your right, pivoting on your right foot. As your opponent tries to take a step with his or her right foot, he or she is literally wheeled over your blocking foot. It is important to get a strong steering-wheel motion going with your arms, as this will help lift the opponent off the ground as he or she tumbles over your foot. This technique requires great timing, but can be dynamic when done properly.

KOSHI-WAZA: HIP THROWS

Hip throws describe a technique where an opponent is rotated, or wheeled, over your hip. Opponents are lifted onto your hip and then thrown with a variety of sweeping, wheeling, or rotating movements. These are big powerful throws that look spectacular when performed at speed.

O-GOSHI: MAJOR HIP THROW

The major hip throw forms the basis for most hip throws. Once this technique has been learned, there are many adaptations and variations that can be derived from it. Traditional major hip throws are not common in competitions, but the basic principles behind them are seen in competitions all over the world.

Although you can start from a conventional (low-sleeve) grip, the major hip throw uses a different grip to actually throw. As you take a step forward with your right foot, release your right-handed lapel grip, and slip your arm underneath your opponent's left armpit and around his

Unlike most combat sports, judo has a strong female participation, and women's judo can be as spectacular as the men's. Spain's Olympic champion, Isabel Fernandez, wins the 2001 European Championships here with this throw.

MAJOR HIP THROW

STEP 1: The attacker steps forward with his right foot, placing it between his opponent's feet.

STEP 2: Pivoting on his right foot, he brings his left foot level with it and bends his knees to lift his opponent.

STEP 3: As he straightens his legs and rotates his body, his opponent is lifted off the floor.

back. Try to grip his or her belt for extra power, but if you cannot, just hug your opponent, or grab the back of his or her jacket.

Pivoting on the ball of your right foot and pulling hard with your left hand on your opponent's sleeve, bring your left foot in beside your right, and bend your knees. Just as with the shoulder throw, as you straighten your knees, your opponent will be lifted off the mat and onto your hip. Now complete the throw by rotating your head and upper body to the left as you continue to pull hard on your opponent's sleeve.

There are many variations on the hip throw. These include harai-goshi (sweeping hip throw) and uki-goshi (floating hip throw), both of which use a variety of different grips and foot positions. If you can master the major hip throw first, the others will be a lot easier to learn.

KOSHI-GURUMA: HIP WHEEL

This hip throw involves more of a rotation movement than most of the others. It is ideal for taller fighters who can easily wrap their arm around a shorter person's neck.

From a conventional grip, step forward with your right foot, just as with the other hip throws. But this time, throw your right arm around your opponent's neck, securing control of his or her head. As you pivot on your right foot and bring your left foot in next to it, thrust your hips to the right across your opponent's body.

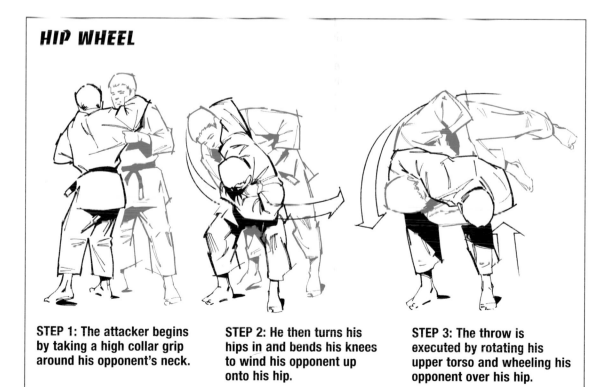

HIP WHEEL

STEP 1: The attacker begins by taking a high collar grip around his opponent's neck.

STEP 2: He then turns his hips in and bends his knees to wind his opponent up onto his hip.

STEP 3: The throw is executed by rotating his upper torso and wheeling his opponent over his hip.

There is much less knee bend on this throw than in the others. Now complete the throw by rotating your body to your left and wheeling your opponent over your hip.

It is important to have good control over your opponent's head with this technique, otherwise he or she can easily resist your rotating motion. It is difficult to perform this throw without following through and landing on your opponent, making it a devastating throw.

UCHI-MATA: INNER THIGH THROW

The inner thigh throw is probably the most impressive and fluent technique in judo. In fact, a perfectly executed inner thigh throw is

INNER THIGH THROW

STEP 1: The attacker steps forward into the space between his opponent's legs, creating space for his lifting leg.

STEP 2: He then pivots on his right foot and, swiveling his hips, brings his left foot in between his opponent's.

STEP 3: The throw is completed by sweeping backwards with his right leg and lifting with his left.

probably the most graceful sight in judo. Many great champions are uchi-mata experts.

This throw requires great spring in the legs. It is good for shorter fighters who can easily get underneath an opponent. Although it is often considered a leg or foot-sweep technique, this technique uses movements that are actually similar to those used in the hip throws. It is usually best to do the inner thigh throw from a high right-handed grip, as this gives you more control over your opponent's head. It is also important to have a low-sleeve grip.

The inner thigh throw is usually done in a three-step movement. As in the major hip throw, begin with a forward step using your right foot, a body twist (turning your body to face the same way as your opponent), and a strong pull on the sleeve. As you bring your left foot next to your right, it is important to place it deep between your opponent's legs and to bend the knee as much as possible. In a flowing movement, you then sweep backwards with your right leg as you straighten your left leg, lifting your opponent off the ground. The outside of your right thigh brushes against the inside of your opponent's right thigh as you sweep him or her off the ground. The throw is completed with the rotation of your head and your upper body.

SUTEMI-WAZA: SACRIFICIAL TECHNIQUES

Sacrificial techniques are mostly performed as counter techniques against an opponent's attack, but they can also be done as attacking moves. A sacrificial technique is a technique in which you throw yourself to the ground in order to throw your opponent.

Sacrificial throws require an attacker to throw him- or herself down onto the mat to throw an opponent. Here, the U.S.'s Jimmy Pedro attempts a sacrificial throw on his way to winning the 1999 World Championships.

VALLEY DROP

STEP 1: The attacker pulls his opponent in tightly by grabbing his jacket around the back.

STEP 2: He then swivels around his opponent and throws his left leg behind his opponent's legs.

STEP 3: By keeping a tight grip and sitting down, the attacker takes his opponent over backwards.

TANI-OTOSHI: VALLEY DROP

The valley drop is rarely used as a straightforward attack; it is almost always used as a counterattacking method when your opponent turns his or her back on you, possibly attempting a hip throw.

If you wish to use this technique to attack your opponent, however, you should start with a conventional grip and a wide foot base. Bring your right foot in to meet your left foot as you pull your opponent in tightly. Now swing your left leg around the back of your opponent's legs and flop down onto your bottom. Your left leg will block your opponent from stepping backwards. If you have him or her pulled in tightly enough, the weight of your body dropping down will pull him or her backwards, over your outstretched leg.

It is vital to wrap your opponent up tightly. You could try grabbing him or her in a bear hug or grip him or her under the armpits or behind the

STOMACH THROW

STEP 1: The attacker steps backwards to create space between himself and his opponent.

STEP 2: He lifts his foot up to his opponent's stomach and sits down as close to his feet as possible.

STEP 3: By keeping a tight grip on his opponent's jacket, he levers him over his outstretched leg.

back. Whatever your grip, as long as you hold on tight, your opponent will come crashing down onto the mat.

TOMOE-NAGE: STOMACH THROW

This technique was made famous by the action-thriller film *Goldfinger*, in which the infamous Pussy Galore throws James Bond into a haystack using the stomach throw. This throw can be effective when done properly. It is one of the few sacrificial techniques that is common as an outright attack—although it relies heavily on the element of surprise.

This technique can be equally performed with a conventional, double-lapel, or double-sleeve grip. From your grip, take a step forward with your left foot, placing it between your opponent's legs

58

while pulling with both hands to draw your opponent forward. Bring your right foot up to your opponent's stomach, and sit down as close to your own left heel as you can. Pulling your opponent onto you with your arms, rotate him or her over the top of your head by guiding him or her with your outstretched leg. It is important to pull your opponent's upper body in close to prevent him or her from doing a cartwheel out of the throw. You can also follow through into a hold by letting your opponent's momentum carry you over so that you land on top of him or her.

YOKO-GURUMA: SIDE WHEEL

Like the valley drop, the side wheel is almost exclusively a counterattacking technique. It is commonly used against hip

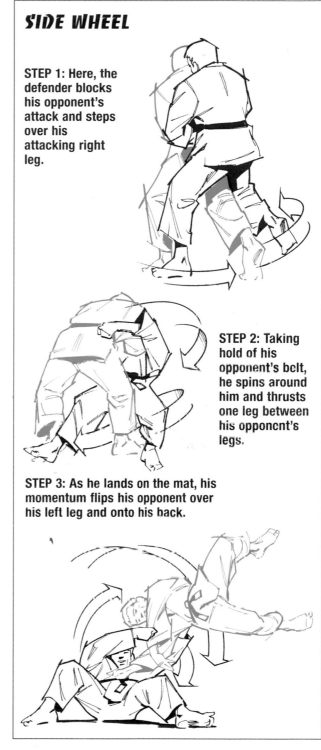

SIDE WHEEL

STEP 1: Here, the defender blocks his opponent's attack and steps over his attacking right leg.

STEP 2: Taking hold of his opponent's belt, he spins around him and thrusts one leg between his opponent's legs.

STEP 3: As he lands on the mat, his momentum flips his opponent over his left leg and onto his back.

throws or arm techniques in which the opponent has turned his or her back on you. Sink your hips and pull backwards to block your opponent's attack.

Now wrap your left arm around his or her waist (preferably grabbing the belt) while keeping your right hand on his or her lapel. Step over his or her right leg with your right leg and swing it between your opponent's legs. As you do so, rotate your body around your opponent and throw yourself down at his or her feet. Keeping a strong grip on his or her belt with your left hand, your weight and momentum will drag your opponent over your left leg and left shoulder as you lie on your back.

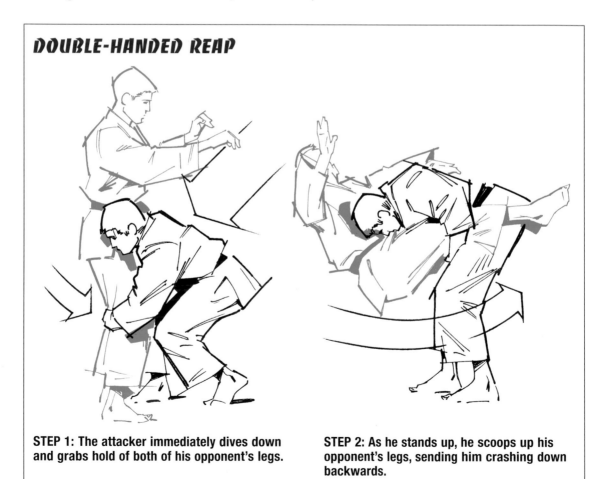

DOUBLE-HANDED REAP

STEP 1: The attacker immediately dives down and grabs hold of both of his opponent's legs.

STEP 2: As he stands up, he scoops up his opponent's legs, sending him crashing down backwards.

Pick-up techniques require great explosive power. Estonia's Alexsei Budolin is one of the world's best pick-up specialists and won the 2001 Moscow Grand Prix finals with a series of devastating pick-ups like this one.

This is a difficult sacrifice throw and requires great speed and commitment. The slightest hesitation will result in you being buried by your opponent.

PICK-UP TECHNIQUES

In modern judo, pick-ups are the most vigorous and breathtaking techniques and are different from all the other techniques. While the principle of judo is to use minimum force and maximum efficiency, pick-ups are the exception to this rule, as they require great upper-body strength to perform.

MOROTE-GARI: DOUBLE-HANDED REAP

The double-handed reap is the simplest form of pick-up. It is usually performed as a surprise attack before you even take hold of your opponent. As your opponent steps forward to meet you, bend down (from your knees), and grab both of his or her legs behind the knees or thighs. Pull his or her legs in tight as you straighten up and drive him or her backwards with your shoulder.

Typically, an opponent will have leaned quite far over you as you bend down, and so it will be necessary to lift him or her right off the ground and throw him or her to one side.

URA-NAGE: REAR THROW

The rear throw is a bone-crunching technique that requires immense strength. It is commonly used as a counterattacking technique, but it can also sometimes be used in a straight attack.

From a conventional grip, step around with your left foot and place it just behind your opponent, sinking your hips as you do so. At the same time, let

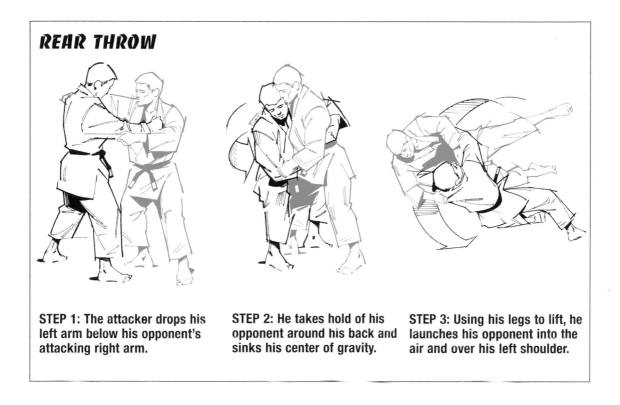

REAR THROW

STEP 1: The attacker drops his left arm below his opponent's attacking right arm.

STEP 2: He takes hold of his opponent around his back and sinks his center of gravity.

STEP 3: Using his legs to lift, he launches his opponent into the air and over his left shoulder.

go of the sleeve grip, and wrap your left arm around your opponent's waist, securing a grip on his or her belt, if possible. With one foot in front and one behind your opponent and with a low position and a tight grip, you are now ready to lift your opponent. Lift with your legs, straightening up as you do so, and heave your opponent onto your left hip. With your opponent fully off the ground, twist around to the left, and take him or her over backwards. In the most spectacular rear throws, the player thrown can be lifted shoulder-high in the air before coming crashing down onto his or her back.

KATA-GURUMA: SHOULDER WHEEL

This is essentially a fireman's lift and requires great strength in the legs —a favorite technique for powerful "scrappers" rather than elegant technicians.

SHOULDER WHEEL

STEP 1: The attacker stoops down and takes hold of the inside of his opponent's thigh.

STEP 2: He pulls him across his shoulder with his other hand and lifts him up by straightening his legs.

STEP 3: He continues the wheeling motion by pulling down with his left hand and letting go with his right.

From a standard grip, release your right hand and step forward with your right foot, crouching as you do so, and twisting your body to face your opponent's side. Thrust your right arm between your opponent's legs, and grab hold of his or her left thigh while pulling down with your left hand on his or her sleeve, so you can pull him or her across your shoulders. From this position, lift your opponent up into the fireman's lift by straightening your legs; it is important to bend from the knees rather than from the back to avoid injury. As you lift your opponent off the ground, continue pulling down with your left hand and push up with your right arm. This will continue your opponent's forward momentum so that he or she does not stop on your shoulders, but is flipped over your shoulders and onto the mat.

When practicing this technique, do so from your knees so that you do not drop your opponent from a great height. Also, you must never let go of your opponent's left sleeve, as this can help control his or her fall.

NE-WAZA: GROUND TECHNIQUES

Once a throw has been attempted, a judo contest may move into the groundwork stage, unless the throw is awarded a perfect score. In groundwork, there are three elements: osaekomi-waza (a hold), shime-waza (a strangle or choke), and kansetsu-waza (an armlock).

If a throw does not end in a perfect score, the contest can move into a battle on the ground. Here, France's Stephane Traineau secures a winning hold on his way to a bronze medal at the 2000 Sydney Olympics.

SCARF HOLD

The attacker pins his opponent by securing the top of his body by wrapping up his head and arm.

The transitional period between standing fighting and groundwork is just as vital as the throw and ground techniques themselves. Swift transference from standing into groundwork can often make the difference between winning and losing.

There are three ways to win on the ground: by pinning your opponent in a hold for 25 seconds; by forcing your opponent to submit using a strangle; or by forcing a submission from an armlock position. Strangles and armlocks are the quickest ways to gain a victory on the ground, but they are prohibited in junior competitions for safety reasons. Juniors can still learn these techniques, but will have to wait until they are seniors to use them in competition.

The International Judo Federation lists 9 different holds, 11 strangles and chokes, and 9 armlocks. Following are three examples of each category.

HOLDS (OSAEKOMI-WAZA)

Once a contest moves onto the ground, the simplest way to gain a victory is to pin your opponent on his or her back and hold him or her there for the allotted time, 25 seconds. An opponent does not have to be held entirely on his or her back, but his shoulders must be immobilized and you must be pinning your opponent from above. There are various ways to escape a hold, such as twisting onto your front, trapping one or both of your opponent's legs, and dragging both you and your opponent outside the competition area.

KESA-GATAME: SCARF HOLD

The scarf hold is almost always the first ground technique taught to beginners. This is because it is the easiest hold to follow into after throwing with a hip throw—or any technique that requires a high-collar grip.

This hold is simple, but powerful. With your opponent lying flat on his or her back, approach from his or her left side. Pick up his or her right arm and tuck it under your left armpit. Leaning the right side of your ribcage across your opponent's chest, wrap your right arm around the back of his or her neck. Spread your legs into a hurdle position, with your right leg forward and your left leg tucked behind you. Your bottom should be tucked up tightly against your opponent's side; your right side should be across his or her chest; and your head should be kept down over his or her right shoulder. From here, it is important to squeeze tightly in order to restrict your opponent's ability to wriggle or struggle.

There are two variations of the scarf hold: kuzure-kesa-gatame (broken scarf hold) and ushiro-kesa-gatame (reverse scarf hold). In the broken hold, you have your right arm tucked underneath your opponent's left armpit rather than around the back of his or her neck. In the reverse hold, your body position is identical to the scarf hold, but facing the opposite direction

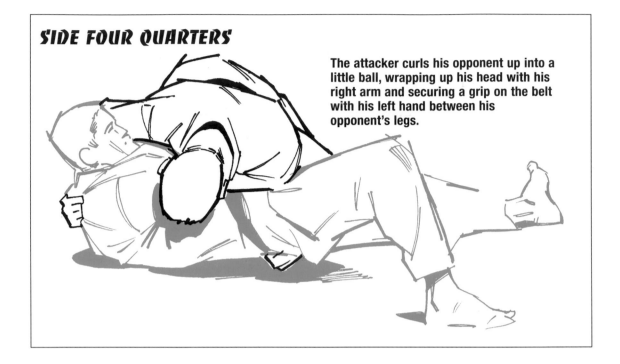

SIDE FOUR QUARTERS

The attacker curls his opponent up into a little ball, wrapping up his head with his right arm and securing a grip on the belt with his left hand between his opponent's legs.

(towards your opponent's feet), so that your right arm is tucked down his or her side rather than around his or her neck.

YOKO-SHIHO-GATAME: SIDE FOUR QUARTERS

The side four quarters hold wraps up your opponent into a tight ball, making it difficult for him or her to wriggle free. It would typically be applied after you had thrown your opponent using a technique that involves grabbing his or her leg, or after rolling your opponent over from his or her front using his or her leg.

Approaching from your opponent's left side, lean forwards over his or her torso. Wrap your right arm around the back of his or her neck, and take hold of his or her jacket around the shoulder. Your left arm goes between his or her legs, and your left hand should try to grip his or her belt around his or her right hip. The closer you can get your hands together, the better, as your opponent will be in an even tighter ball. If you can link your hands together, the hold will be almost inescapable. Your legs can be either stretched out behind you, with your hips pushed down to the mat, or you can sit back on your knees. Sitting back on your knees will help pull your opponent in tightly towards you, but stretching out your legs will give you more versatility in reacting to your opponent's struggles.

A variation on this technique, called kuzure-yoko-shiho-gatame, is similar, but rather than wrapping your right arm around your opponent's neck, you trap his or her far shoulder.

KAMI-SHIHO-GATAME: UPPER FOUR QUARTERS

The upper four quarters hold is usually applied after you have thrown your opponent over your head and he or she has landed with his or her head facing you.

Approach your opponent from his or her head, and then lean forwards over his or her upper chest. Put your arms outside his arms, and tuck your hands in under his elbows. From there, try to hold your opponent's belt, as this will help you tie his or her

UPPER FOUR QUARTERS

The attacker secures the top half of his opponent's body by tying his arms in by holding his opponent's belt.

arms in tightly against his or her body. The top of your chest should be pressing against the top of your opponent's chest, with your head resting around his or her solar plexus. Keep your elbows pushed in tightly and your legs in the same position as the side four quarters hold: either spread out behind you, or tucked up tightly against your opponent's shoulders.

The upper four quarters hold is particularly effective, as it involves trapping your opponent's arms so that he or she cannot use them to squirm free. Your opponent cannot bridge (arcing your back off the mat by pushing up with your shoulders and the balls of your feet) either, as you have your body weight over the top of his or her torso.

Strangles are submission techniques that instantly bring an end to a contest. The U.S.'s Brian Olsen attempts a strangle using his opponent's collar here, on his way to winning the 2001 British Open title.

SAFETY AT PRACTICE

When practicing any judo techniques, you should always remember to release your partner immediately as soon as he or she submits (which he or she will signal by tapping)—even if you do not think that you performed the technique correctly. This is especially true when practicing choke or strangle techniques. The most important thing when practicing any judo technique is the safety of both you and your partner.

One variation of this hold, called kuzure-kami-shiho-gatame, is done with one or both of your arms tucked inside your opponent's arms, with your elbows tucked under his or her armpits. This is not as strong a hold as the four quarters hold proper, however, as your opponent will be able to use one or both arms to try to roll you over, or to help push him- or herself away from you.

There are a variety of other holds, such as the kata-gatame (shoulder hold) and the tate-shiho-gatame (trunk hold). In each of these holds, the principle of pinning the upper body is the same. As long as you can immobilize your opponent's shoulders, keep your weight evenly balanced across his or her upper torso, and stabilize yourself with your legs, he or she should not be able to escape.

SHIME-WAZA: STRANGLES AND CHOKES

The basic principle of a strangle or choke is to block either your opponent's blood circulation to his or her brain so he or she passes out, or to block his or her windpipe so that he or she cannot breathe. Crude they may be, but these techniques can be effective in a fight.

HADAKA-JIME: NAKED CHOKE

Approaching your opponent from behind (it does not matter which position he or she is in), put your right arm across his or her throat. Make sure that the bony part of your wrist is pressed up against his or her Adam's apple. Take hold of your right hand with your left hand, and pull it towards you, making sure to lean in with your right shoulder against the back of your opponent's neck. The choke will be effective instantly. You can also perform this choke by holding your left bicep (instead of your left hand) with your right hand and putting your left hand behind your opponent's

NAKED CHOKE

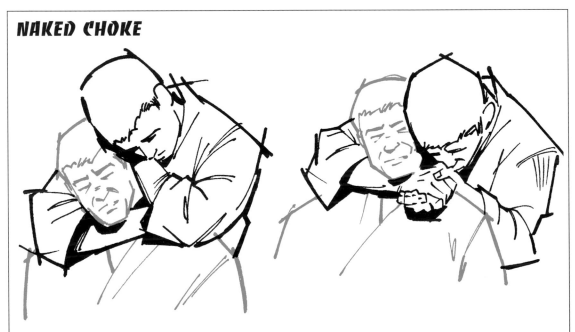

STEP 1: The attacker uses his own elbow to lever pressure against his opponent's throat by pushing against the back of his opponent's head.

STEP 2: The attacker uses his shoulder to put pressure against the back of his opponent's head and clasps his hands to pull against the throat.

SINGLE-WING STRANGLE

The attacker pulls his opponent's collar across his throat with his right hand and holds the back of his collar with his left, putting pressure against his jugular.

head. This is an even more effective choke than the original, but it takes longer to apply.

KATA-HAJIME: SINGLE-WING STRANGLE

Like the naked choke, this strangle can be done from any position: standing, kneeling, lying on top of your opponent's back, or underneath him or her. This technique is most effective when your opponent is defending him- or herself by curling up into a ball, thus stopping you from rolling him or her over onto his or her back.

Approaching your opponent from behind, put your right arm across his or her throat. Extend your thumb as deep into his or her collar as you can, and grab tightly onto the lapel. With your left arm, scoop up your opponent's left arm, and extend your arm under his or her armpit and across the back of his or her neck, forcing his or her left arm up in the air as you do so.

The strangle is applied by pulling down sharply with your right hand and pushing your opponent's head forwards with your left. This action will force your opponent's rough jacket collar against his or her carotid artery in the side of his or her neck, causing him or her to feel faint. It also applies

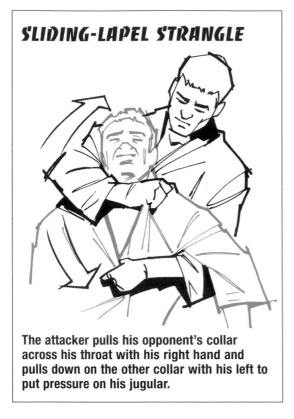

SLIDING-LAPEL STRANGLE

The attacker pulls his opponent's collar across his throat with his right hand and pulls down on the other collar with his left to put pressure on his jugular.

pressure to your opponent's windpipe, thus choking as well as strangling him or her.

In groundwork situations, you should try to trap your opponent with your legs while applying the strangle to stop him or her from escaping. This is particularly important if you are lying beneath your opponent.

OKURI-ERI-JIME: SLIDING-LAPEL STRANGLE

This strangle begins in a similar position to the single-wing strangle. It uses the same principles, and is usually attempted from similar positions.

Start by sliding your right hand across your opponent's throat, with your thumb deep inside his or her lapel. Pass your left arm underneath his or her armpit, and then reach across to his or her far (right-hand) lapel. Putting your thumb inside the lapel, pull it downwards, also pulling down with your right hand. This action will put pressure on both sides of your opponent's neck, blocking the artery on both sides and making him or her feel uncomfortable. This strangle comes on quickly, and is uncomfortable for your opponent, so you should always be ready to release it quickly at practice.

Most of the strangles and chokes involve the use of your opponent's lapel to put pressure on his or her neck. There is also one strangle that is performed using the legs, but it is advanced and is rarely taught to juniors or beginners.

KANSETSU-WAZA: ARMLOCKS

Armlocks involve putting pressure on your opponent's elbow joint and forcing

him or her to submit by tapping. Shoulder locks are illegal in judo and it is important to perform armlocks properly or you could be disqualified from competition for an illegal lock. You can use any part of your body to apply an armlock, as long as it puts pressure on your opponent's elbow joint. Indeed, most armlocks require the use of several parts of the body to effect. It is difficult to apply an armlock using just your hands. Therefore, it is usually necessary to use

Armlocks are used to gain submissions by putting pressure against the elbow joint. Germany's Martin Schmidt forces a submission here against his Danish opponent.

75

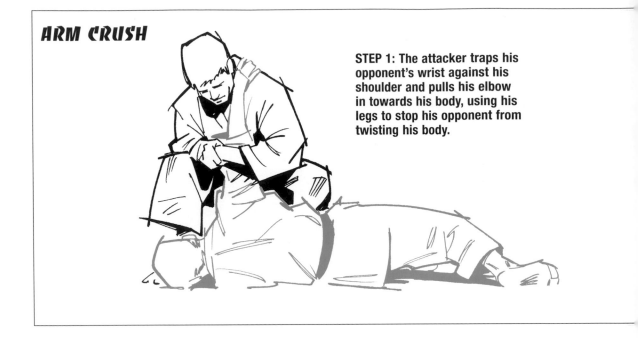

ARM CRUSH

STEP 1: The attacker traps his opponent's wrist against his shoulder and pulls his elbow in towards his body, using his legs to stop his opponent from twisting his body.

another part of your body to put pressure on the elbow. Traditionally, judo also has leg locks, but these have been banned because they are too dangerous to do in competition.

The principle of an armlock is to immobilize your opponent by locking his or her elbow and hence stop him or her from attacking you. Although these can cause damage to someone's elbow ligaments, or even a breakage, armlocks are a highly defensive measure.

UDE-GATAME: ARM CRUSH

The arm crush can either be done from a standing position or from the ground. It is easiest, however, to practice this technique while on your knees, with your opponent lying down side-on to you. This technique can either be used for a counterattack or as a method of straight attack. It is also useful when your opponent is trying to fend you off with a straight arm.

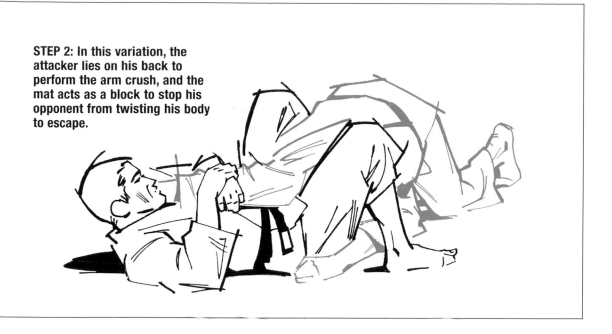

STEP 2: In this variation, the attacker lies on his back to perform the arm crush, and the mat acts as a block to stop his opponent from twisting his body to escape.

From your opponent's high-sleeve grip, trap his or her palm against your collarbone. Next pull his or her arm straight, and then place both hands on his or her elbow joint. Leaning in to your opponent's hand with your shoulder, pull his or her elbow in towards you. This action will put immediate pressure on your opponent's elbow joint and will thus force him or her to submit.

You can try this armlock from a lying-down position on your back, with your opponent between your legs, or you can try it from a standing position. The principle is the same in either case: Simply trap his or her hand against your shoulder, and then crush the elbow joint by pulling it towards you. Just like the strangles and chokes, however, you must be ready to let go the moment your partner taps his or her submission signal, or you could cause serious ligament damage in his or her elbow—or even a fracture of the bone.

UDE-GARAMI: FIGURE-FOUR ARMLOCK

This position makes a figure of four, which is how the technique acquired its name. The figure-four armlock is another technique that can be applied from a variety of different positions, but it is usually performed when you are on top of your opponent while fighting on the ground. The figure-four armlock can be done using only one arm, but it is considerably easier and more powerful to use both.

When your opponent is lying flat on his or her back, approach him or her from his or her left side. Lean over his or her body, and take hold of his or her right wrist with your right hand. Pull it up above his or her elbow, forcing him or her to bend his or her arm. Slip your left arm underneath his or her upper arm, and take hold of your own right wrist. To apply the armlock, pull his or her wrist in towards his or her own shoulder, and roll your own wrists forward. This tightens the pressure on your opponent's joint, and usually results in a quick submission. It is important to control your opponent by lying across his or her torso to prevent him or her from escaping, however, otherwise the armlock will not work.

JUJI-GATAME: CROSS ARMLOCK

The cross armlock is the most common armlock applied in judo. The reason for its popularity is that it is the quickest technique to drop into after you have thrown someone while standing and your opponent has landed on his or her back.

With your opponent lying on his or her back, stand at his or her left side, with your feet against him or her, and pull his or her left arm up. You should stand with a leg on either side of his or her arm, and pull it straight. Sit straight down, as close in to your opponent as you can, and put your right leg across his or her neck. You can also put your left leg across his or her stomach, but that is not necessary; the right leg across the neck will be enough to stop him or her from twisting away. Making sure that your opponent's palm is facing upward, pull on his or her arm so that his or her elbow joint is resting on one of your hips. Now, lift your hips to apply the lock. You can also push down on his or her palm to help increase the pressure on the joint if the technique does not work right away.

There are a variety of other armlock techniques that use the leg or knee, but in reality, any technique that locks the elbow joint is acceptable. Remember: never attempt an armlock technique while doing a throw. If you attempt any submission technique while performing a throw, you will be instantly disqualified.

FIGURE-FOUR ARMLOCK

The attacker grabs his opponent's wrist with his right hand and his own wrist with his left, and twists them both to perform the armlock.

Training
for Judo

For a local club player, judo training is vastly different from that for a competitive international fighter. Their aims and goals are miles apart, and so, too, is their training regime. The first part of this chapter will cover the kind of training that anyone practicing judo will encounter, while the second part will focus on what it takes to become an elite athlete.

Whatever your level, stretching is absolutely vital before training. Judo is a tough sport, even at relatively low levels, and injuries are common. You can greatly reduce the risk of injury by undergoing a comprehensive warm-up program before you step on the mat. You will begin with a warm-up in any class, but it is always good practice to arrive having already stretched a little yourself.

Anyone who has ever been to exercise classes at school or college will have at least some idea about how to warm up before exercising, but for judo, there are particular areas that you need to concentrate on. Everyone has his or her own preferred system of warming up, but it is usually a good idea to have some form of structure to your warm-up. For example, you might begin warming up at your head and gradually work your way down your

Judo is usually practiced in a dojo among groups of students. When they are practicing, there should always be enough room for each pair to fight freely without bumping into each other.

body. Pay particular attention to your back, as this area takes a lot of strain in judo, and it is easy to pull a muscle. Be sure to warm up your knees, ankles, toes, wrists, and fingers; these are all areas that are easy to forget, yet they take a lot of stress during judo practice.

Once you have stretched, a warm-up will often involve some jogging around the mat to get your heart working and then some push-ups, sit-ups, squats, and skips to make sure that your muscles are nice and warm.

TECHNIQUE TRAINING

Standard training will involve **uchi-komi**, which literally means "fitting in."

Judo-ka from around the world develop their own unique styles. Here, a former wrestler, Iran's Kazim Sarikhani, throws Japanese Olympic champion Makoto Takimoto with his own unique technique.

This is where students get a partner and take turns practicing the actions of throwing techniques to the point of executing a throw, but without actually following through with it. Uchi-komi is done to improve technique and speed of entry into a technique, so you will usually do about 10 or 20 repetitions of one technique as fast as you can before swapping over.

Training will involve learning and practicing new techniques as you move up through the grades, but it will also contain combinations of moves and counterattacks. For example, depending on the aim of a particular session, you may go through some combination of throwing techniques or transference from standing to groundwork.

The sessions often end with some practice fighting, or randori, which literally means "catching chaos." This is a "free practice," in which you compete against a partner, trying to beat each other. You can agree beforehand with your partner on how hard you plan on fighting against each other. As this is a "free practice," students tend to use this time to try out techniques that they have learned during a session to see if they can make them work in competition.

These are all basic training methods, and so you will probably encounter them at any judo club in the world. For students who train just once or twice a week, these methods amount to quite a good workout. For those who show particular ability, or who want to fight at the highest level, however, judo training takes on a different complexion.

ACHIEVING PEAK CONDITION

In order to compete in the international arena, your body has to be in peak physical condition. Most top international fighters train full-time with the help of government grants—or, if their national association is wealthy enough, it may pay for their training.

Such people tend to train every day. This does not necessarily mean that they go to the dojo every day, but they will do some form of training every day. This could be jogging, swimming, cycling, weight training, or indeed, any kind of sporting activity, such as kayaking, ball sports, rock climbing, or even racket sports. Every type of training that they engage in, however, will serve a particular purpose.

To reach the top in judo, you need cardiovascular endurance, strength, explosive speed, a sharp mind, and, of course, good technique. The technique training must be done within the dojo, but the other four areas

BENCH PRESS

Bench presses are a good exercise to increase upper-body strength which is vital for pick-up techniques.

PULLEY TRAINING

REVERSE PULLEY: This is used to increase strength in the back muscles and is a good exercise to help develop the pulling action to force opponents to step forward onto your throws.

FORWARD PULLEY: This works the deltoids (shoulder muscles), which is important for techniques such as the shoulder throws, where an opponent is thrown over your head.

can be worked on outside the dojo. Endurance work can be anything like running, cycling, swimming, or any sporting activity, as long as it lasts at least half an hour. You must not waste this time, however, just going through the motions; you must work hard for the duration of the activity. Playing squash is good for stamina, and it is also a thinking game, so it will help keep your mind sharp.

It is good to have a mixture of games, like squash, and pure endurance activities, like running. When you go for a run or when you swim or cycle, use the same circuit on each occasion, and time yourself. That way, you will have a goal to try and beat every time you train.

BICEP CURLS

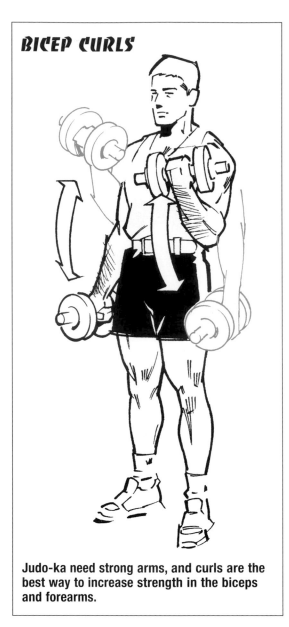

Judo-ka need strong arms, and curls are the best way to increase strength in the biceps and forearms.

INCREASING YOUR STRENGTH

Strength work should be done with specific muscles in mind. It is no good just going to a gym and doing a workout session; you must work on the specific muscles you use for judo. Legs are important, as most of the power in throws comes from them. Squats are good for the legs, but you should also work on your calf muscles, as these will help give you extra spring. Simple exercises, like jumping high in the air, will help you develop explosive speed, as will short sprints or hill sprints.

Although bench presses are a popular exercise in the gym, they are not important for judo, which does not use the chest muscles a great deal. Your shoulders and forearms are the most important muscles for judo, and so these are the ones you should concentrate on. Bicep curls will help build up the forearms, as will wrist curls. To do a bicep curl, hold a dumbbell down by your side with your palm facing forward. Keep your elbow tight against your body and moving your forearm only, pull the dumbbell up toward your shoulder until your

WRIST CURLS

To do a wrist curl, hold a weight in your hands and out in front of you, with your palms facing upwards. Roll the weight to the end of your fingers, and then roll it back into your palms as you curl your wrists toward you. This exercise may feel easy at first, but you will need to do many repetitions in order to get the full benefit.

arm is fully bent. Then slowly straighten your arm again. If you have two dumbbells, you can do each arm alternately, building up a rhythm as you do so. It is best to use relatively light weights and do high repetitions so you build up your anaerobic stamina—which is vital in competitions.

Shoulder machines are common in all gyms, but you will want to try to find ones that require explosive pulling or pushing power. A pulley machine is best, as it works the muscle from a variety of positions: from your elbow being fully bent, to your arm being hyperextended. Lifting a dumbbell above your head from the shoulder also strengthens the muscles.

Push-ups and sit-ups are useful exercises to strengthen your body. They can be done anywhere, and give you a good natural workout. An especially good method of building strength is to do push-ups from your fingertips. This will help strengthen your finger muscles and the muscles around your knuckles. Not only will this improve your grip, but it will also help prevent your fingers from becoming dislocated, another common judo injury.

Grip strength is vital in judo, and thus it is important to work on your forearms. To compete at the highest levels, you need strong gripping

When a competitor peaks for a competition and everything goes to plan, the rewards are great. France's Stephane Traineau was delighted here to win a bronze medal at the 2000 Sydney Olympic Games.

capabilities. A simple exercise to strengthen your forearms is to hold your arms straight out in front of you, clench your fists, and then hyperextend your fingers. Keep doing this for 50 to 100 repetitions. Your arms and fingers will quickly tire, but if you do this every day, your grip will gradually improve.

PUTTING IT ALL TOGETHER

All these exercises will help improve your physical condition, but the main training that will help your judo is randori, or "free practice." You especially need randori to hone your throwing and groundwork skills.

It is no good always fighting the same people or always training at the same club, however. You should travel around and find different people to practice with. People of different weights, sizes, and builds will present you with different challenges. And you should always try to find people better than yourself to be your practice partner. The only way to improve is to test yourself against better opponents, and then try to reach and surpass their levels.

If you cannot find anyone to train with who is better than you, there is still a lot to be learned from weaker opponents. But rather than just going out there and beating your partner quickly and easily, you should limit your own judo to certain techniques or to a certain grip, and try to beat your partner within these limits. No matter how much stronger than your opponent you are, there will always be something you can work on to improve your own judo.

Judo is not just about competing—it should be fun, too. Children, parents, grandparents, men, women—judo is a sport for everyone to enjoy. As long as practicing judo makes you feel happy and confident, that is all you need to keep coming back to your club week after week.

Glossary

Armlock	Pressure applied to the elbow joint
Chui	A five-point penalty; equivalent to yuko
Dan	The denomination of black-belt grades
Dojo	A place where judo is practiced
Feudal	Relating to a social system in which peasants work for a powerful landowner in exchange for food and protection
Ippon	Ten-point score; equivalent to a knockout
Judogi	The judo uniform
Judo-ka	A person who practices judo
Kata	Formal exercises or prearranged sequences of techniques
Keikoku	Seven-point penalty; equal to waza-ari
Koka	Three-point score
Kyu	The denomination of grades from beginner to black belt
Linguist	A person who speaks several languages
Rai	Formal bow
Sake	A Japanese alcoholic drink
Samurai	The warriors of feudal Japan
Shido	Three-point penalty; equivalent to koka
Sumo	A Japanese wrestling martial art
Tatami	Judo mats
Uchi-komi	Fitting in, or technique practice without throwing
Waza-ari	Seven-point score
Yuko	Five-point score

Clothing and Equipment

CLOTHING

Gi: The gi is the most typical martial arts "uniform." Usually in white, but also available in other colors, it consists of a cotton thigh-length jacket and calf-length trousers. Gis come in three weights: light, medium, and heavy. Lightweight gis are cooler than heavyweight gis, but not as strong. The jacket is usually bound at the waist with a belt.

Belt: Belts are used in the martial arts to denote the rank and experience of the wearer. They are made from strong linen or cotton and wrap several times around the body before tying. Beginners usually wear a white belt, and the final belt is almost always black.

Hakama: The hakama is a long folded skirt with five pleats at the front and one at the back. It is a traditional form of clothing in kendo, iaido, and jujutsu.

Zori: A simple pair of slip-on sandals worn in the dojo when not training to keep the floor clean.

WEAPONS

Bokken: A bokken is a long wooden sword made from Japanese oak. Bokken are roughly the same size and shape as a traditional Japanese sword (katana).

Jo: The jo is a simple wooden staff about 4–5 ft (1.3–1.6 m) long and is a traditional weapon of karate and aikido.

Kamma: Two short-handled sickles used as a fighting tool in some types of karate and jujutsu.

Tanto: A wooden knife used for training purposes.

Hojo jutsu: A long rope with a noose on one end used in jujutsu to restrain attackers.

Sai: Long, thin, and sharp spikes, held like knives and featuring wide, spiked handguards just above the handles.

Tonfa: Short poles featuring side handles, like modern-day police batons.

Katana: A traditional Japanese sword with a slightly curved blade and a single, razor-sharp cutting edge.

Butterfly knives: A pair of knives, each one with a wide blade. They are used mainly in kung fu.

Nunchaku: A flail-like weapon consisting of three short sections of staff connected by chains.

Shinai: A bamboo training sword used in the martial art of kendo.

Iaito: A stainless-steel training sword with a blunt blade used in the sword-based martial art of iaido.

TRAINING AIDS

Mook yan jong: A wooden dummy against which the martial artist practices his blocks and punches and conditions his limbs for combat.

Makiwara: A plank of wood set in the ground used for punching and kicking practice.

Focus pads: Circular pads worn on the hands by one person, while his or her partner uses the pads for training accurate punching.

PROTECTIVE EQUIPMENT

Headguard: A padded, protective helmet that protects the wearer from blows to the face and head.

Joint supports: Tight foam or bandage sleeves that go around elbow, knee, or ankle joints and protect the muscles and joints against damage during training.

Groin protector: A well-padded undergarment for men that protects the testicles and the abdomen from kicks and low punches.

Practice mitts: Lightweight boxing gloves that protect the wearer's hands from damage in sparring, and reduce the risk of cuts being inflicted on the opponent.

Chest protector: A sturdy shield worn by women over the chest to protect the breasts during sparring.

Further Reading

Brousse, Michel and David Matsumoto. *Judo—A Sport and a Way of Life.* International Judo Federation, 1999.

Gleeson, Geof. *All About Judo.* Wakefield: E.P. Publishing Ltd, 1975.

Hicks, Simon and Nicolas Soames. *50 Great Judo Champions.* London: Ippon Books, 2001.

Iatskevich, Alexander. *Russian Judo.* London: Ippon Books, 1999.

Leggett, Trevor. *The Dragon Mask and Other Judo Stories in the Zen Tradition.* London: Ippon Books, 1993.

Marwood, Des. *Decisive Judo: Step by Step Introduction.* London: Ippon Books, 1998.

Reay, Tony and Geoffrey Hobbs. *The Judo Manual.* London: Barrie & Jenkins Ltd, 1979.

Yamashita, Yasuhiro. *The Fighting Spirit of Judo.* London: Ippon Books, 1993.

Useful Web Sites

International Judo Federation
http://www.ijf.org

United States Judo Federation
http://www.usjf.com

All Japan Judo Federation
http://www.judo.or.jp

Judo Canada
http://www.judocanada.org

British Judo Association
http://www.britishjudo.org.uk

Judo Federation of Australia
http://www.ausport.gov.au/judo/

Judo New Zealand
http://ourworld.compuserve.com/
homepage/comvirke

Fighting Films
http://www.fightingfilms.com

The World of Judo
http://www.twoj.org

Ippon Books
http://www.ipponbooks.com

About the Author

Barnaby Chesterman is a 1st-dan black belt and has studied judo for more than 20 years. He is the official journalist for the International Judo Federation and has traveled all over the world to cover judo tournaments, including the Olympic Games in Sydney. He is the author of *The Gokyo*, a specialized judo book. He has also participated in taekwondo and Thai boxing, and is a qualified judo coach.

Index

References in italics refer to illustration captions